kwabu

There are more than 25 exciting dinosaurs for you to discover in this coloring book!

We hope you have lots of fun coloring and doodling :-)

_____

Name of the artist

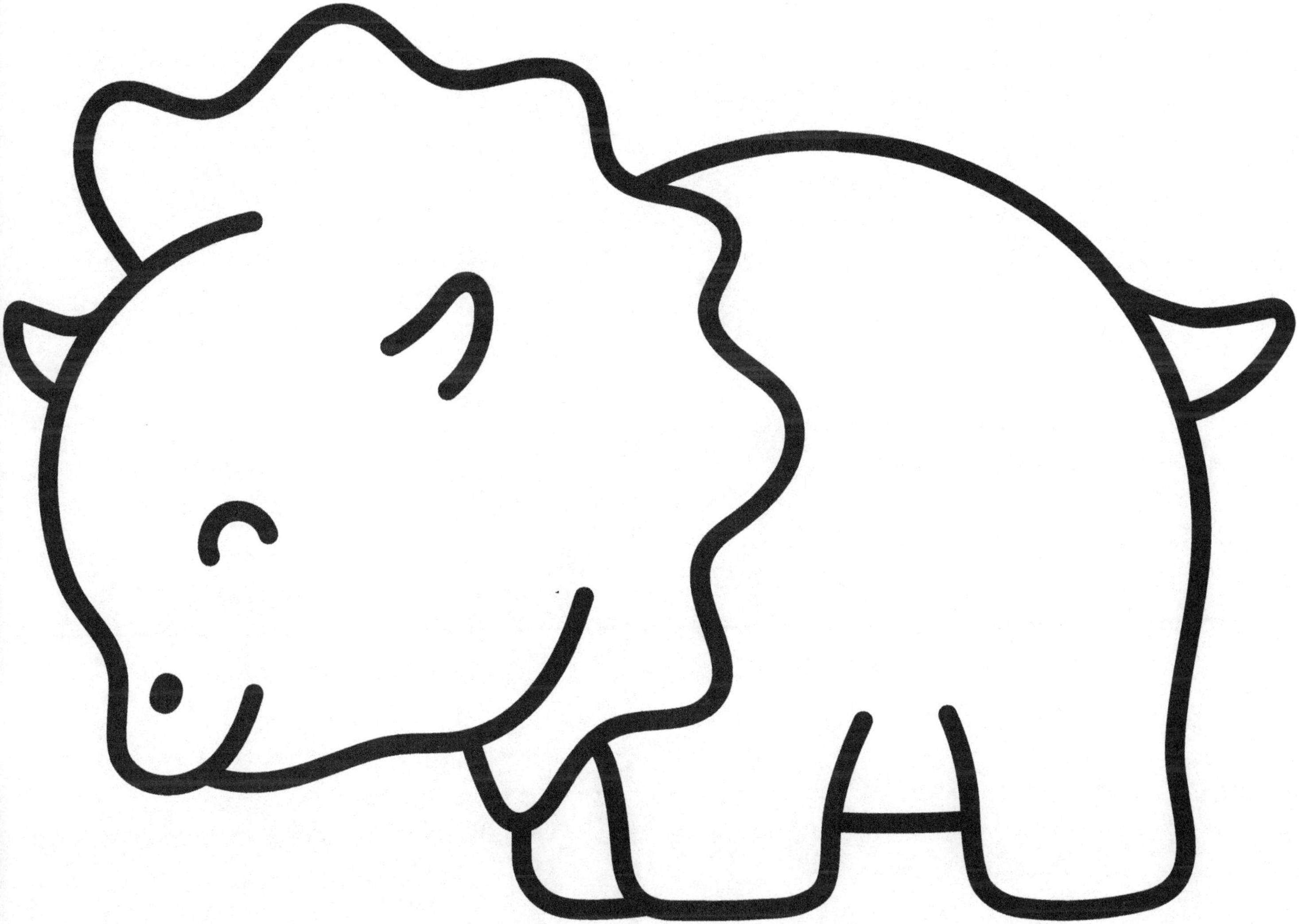

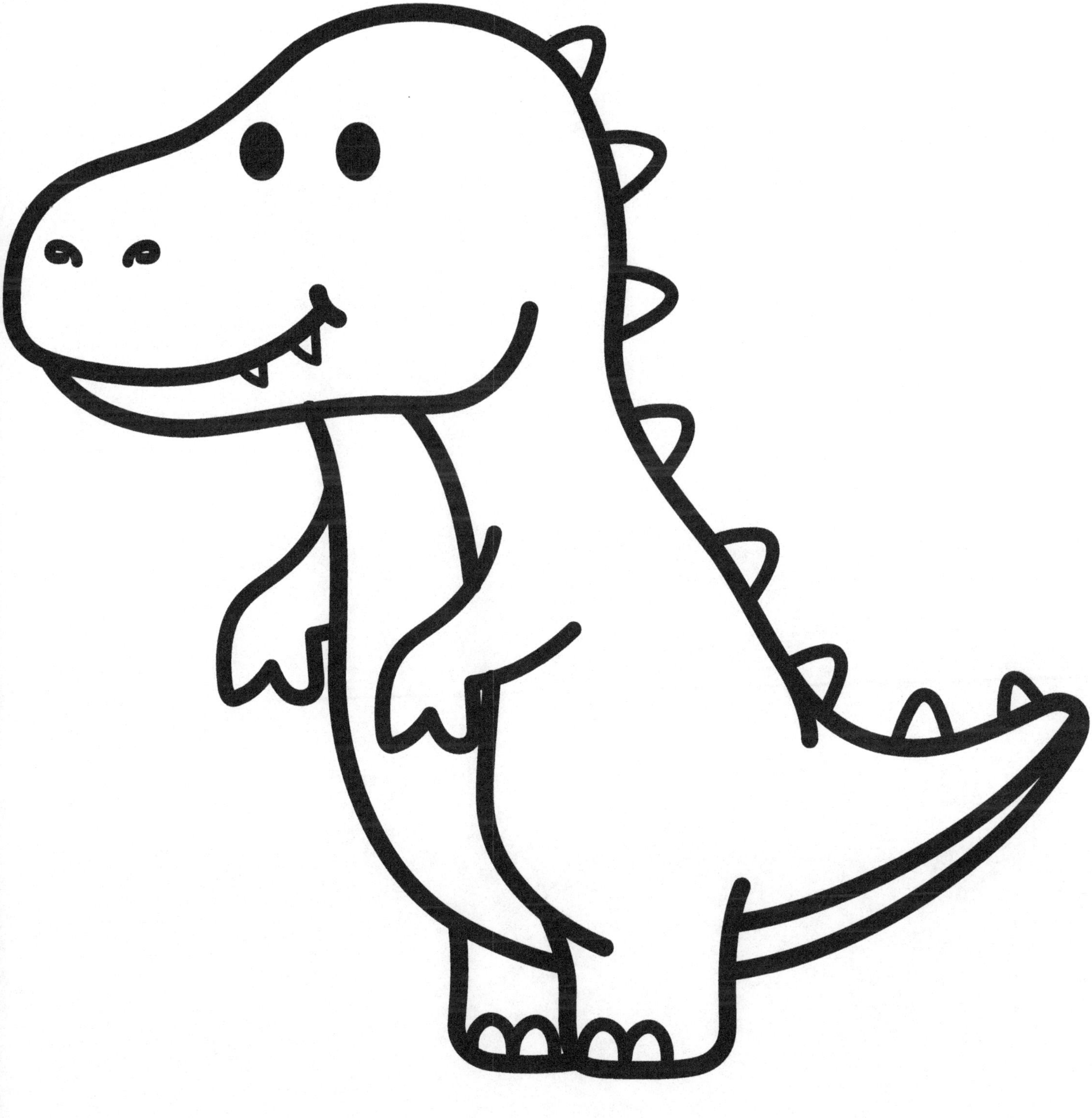

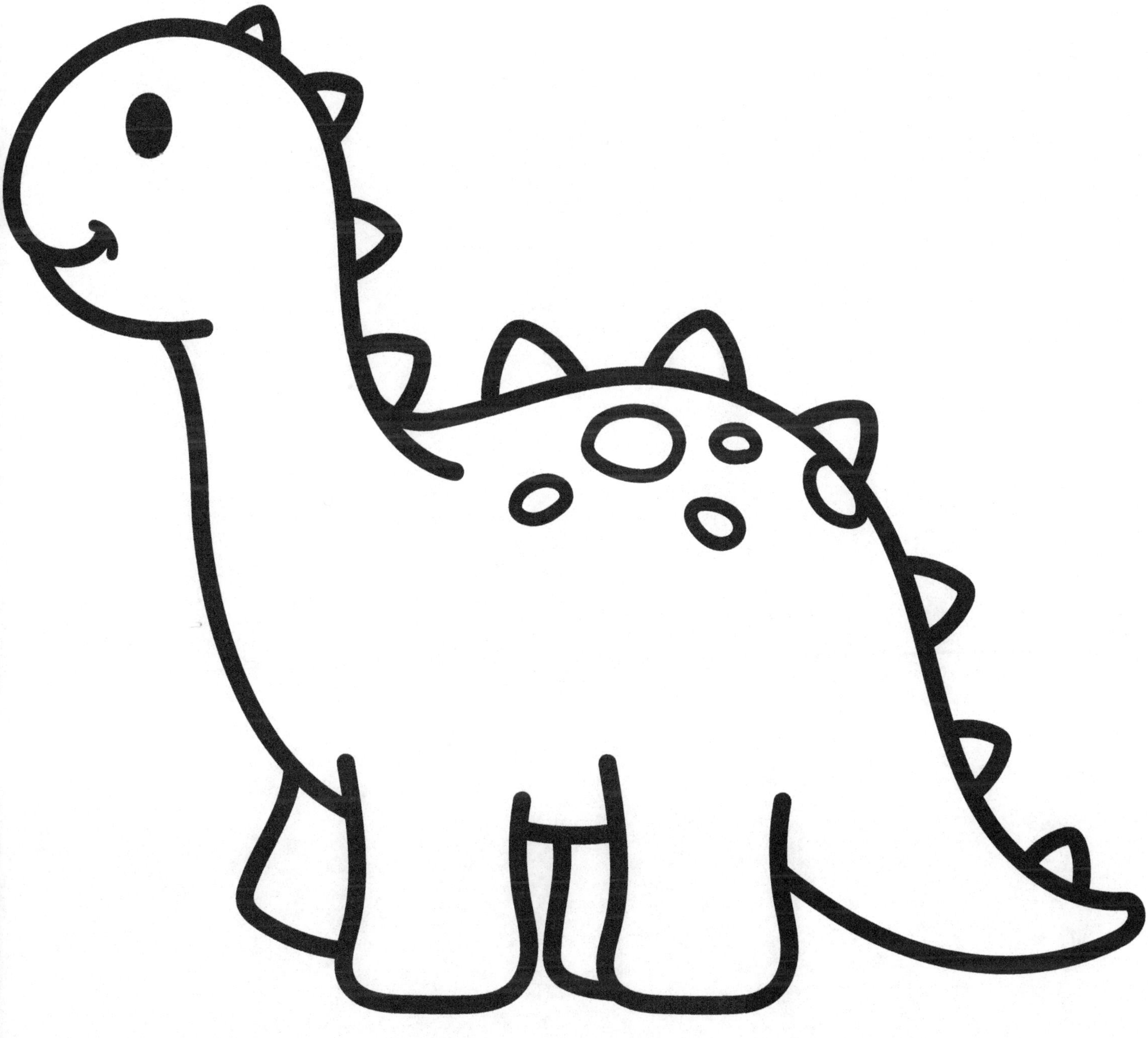

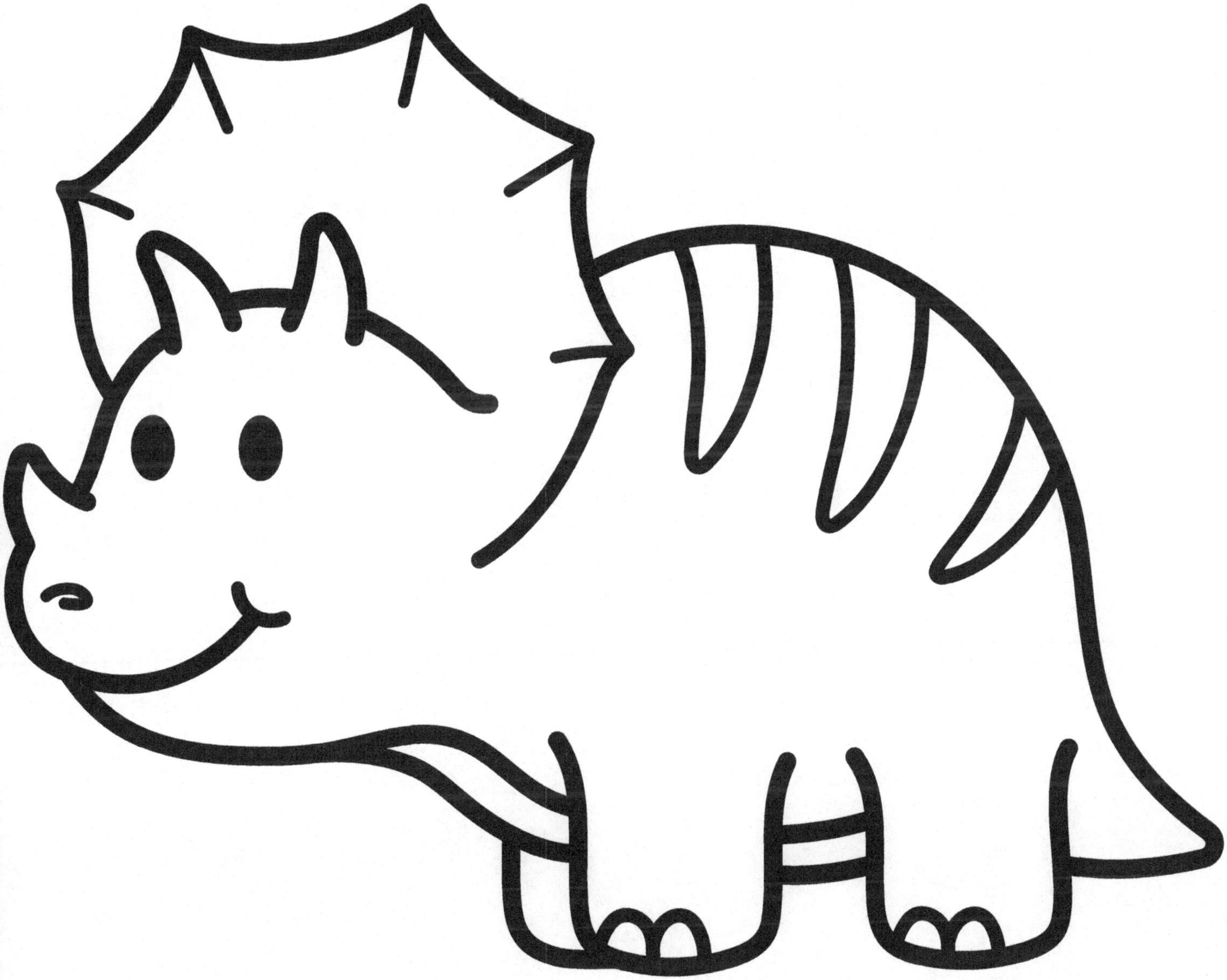

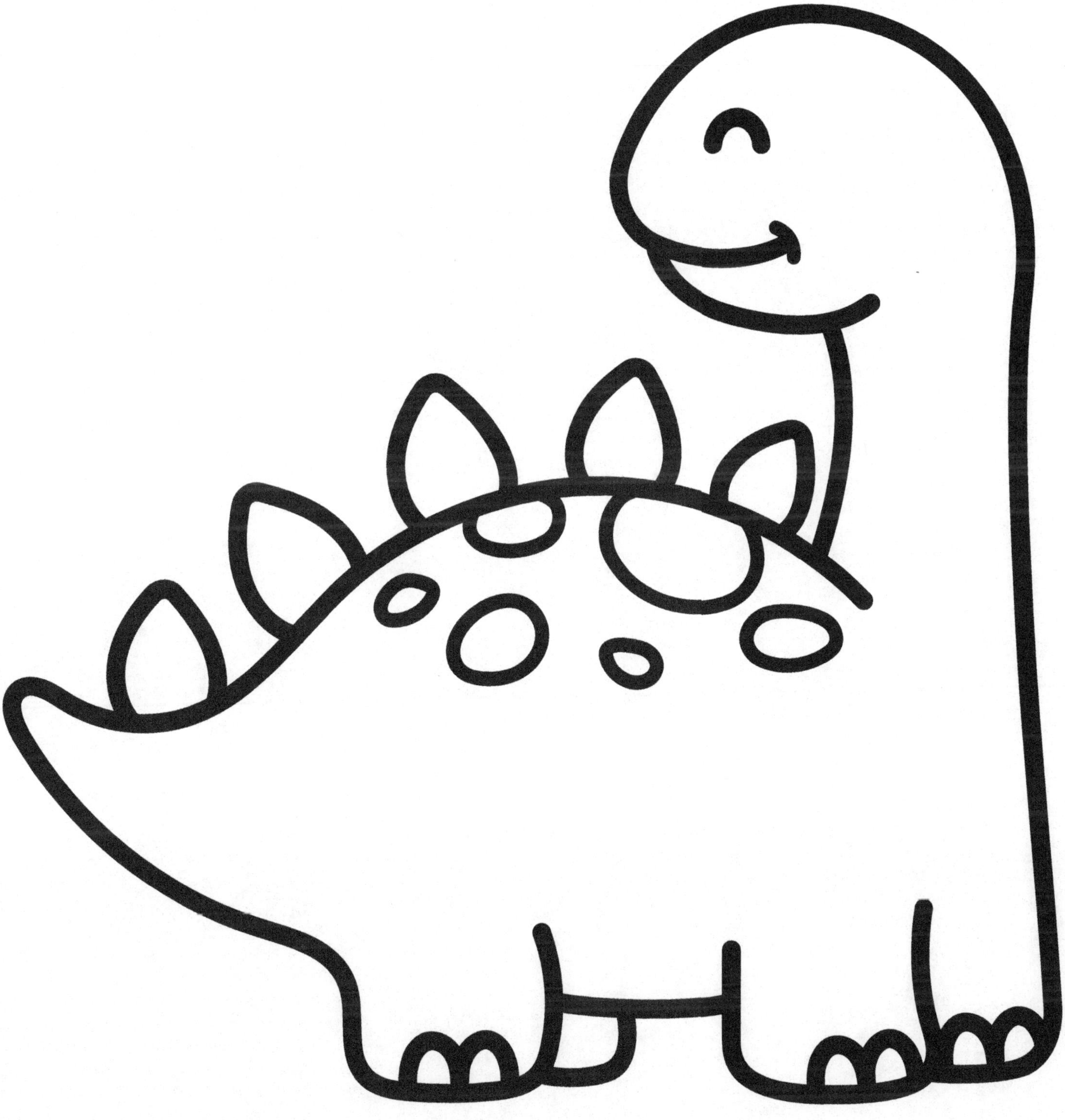

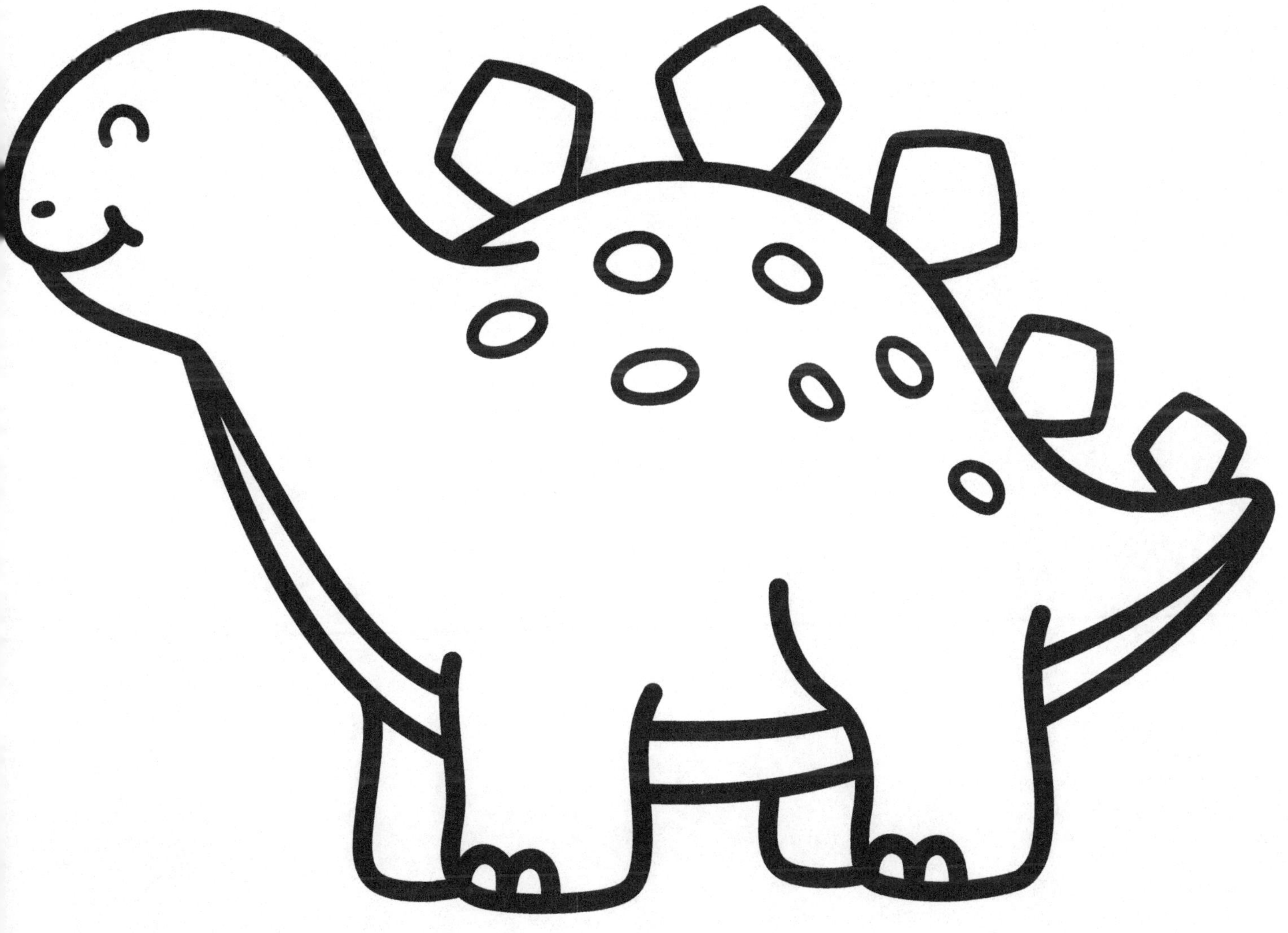

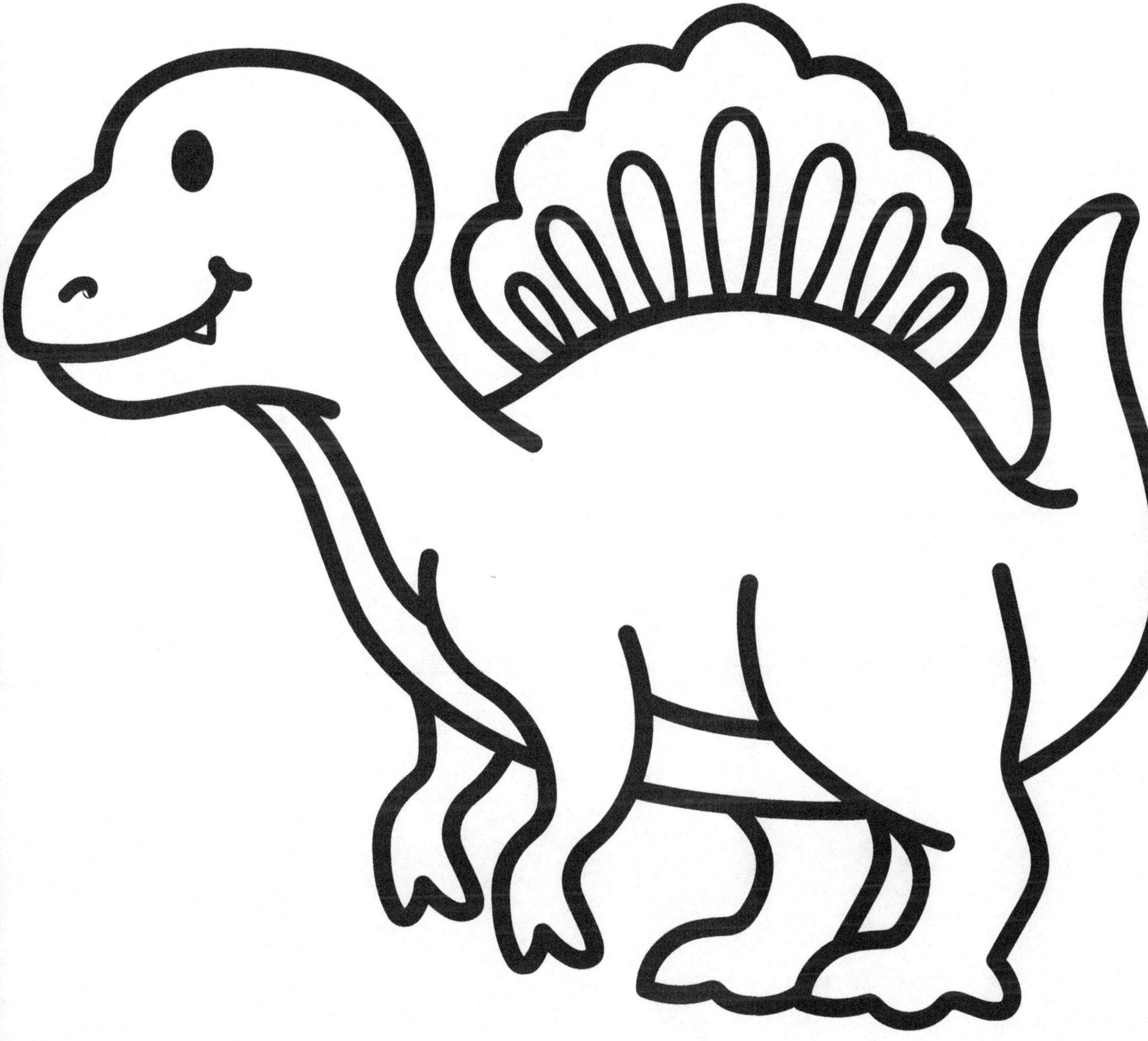

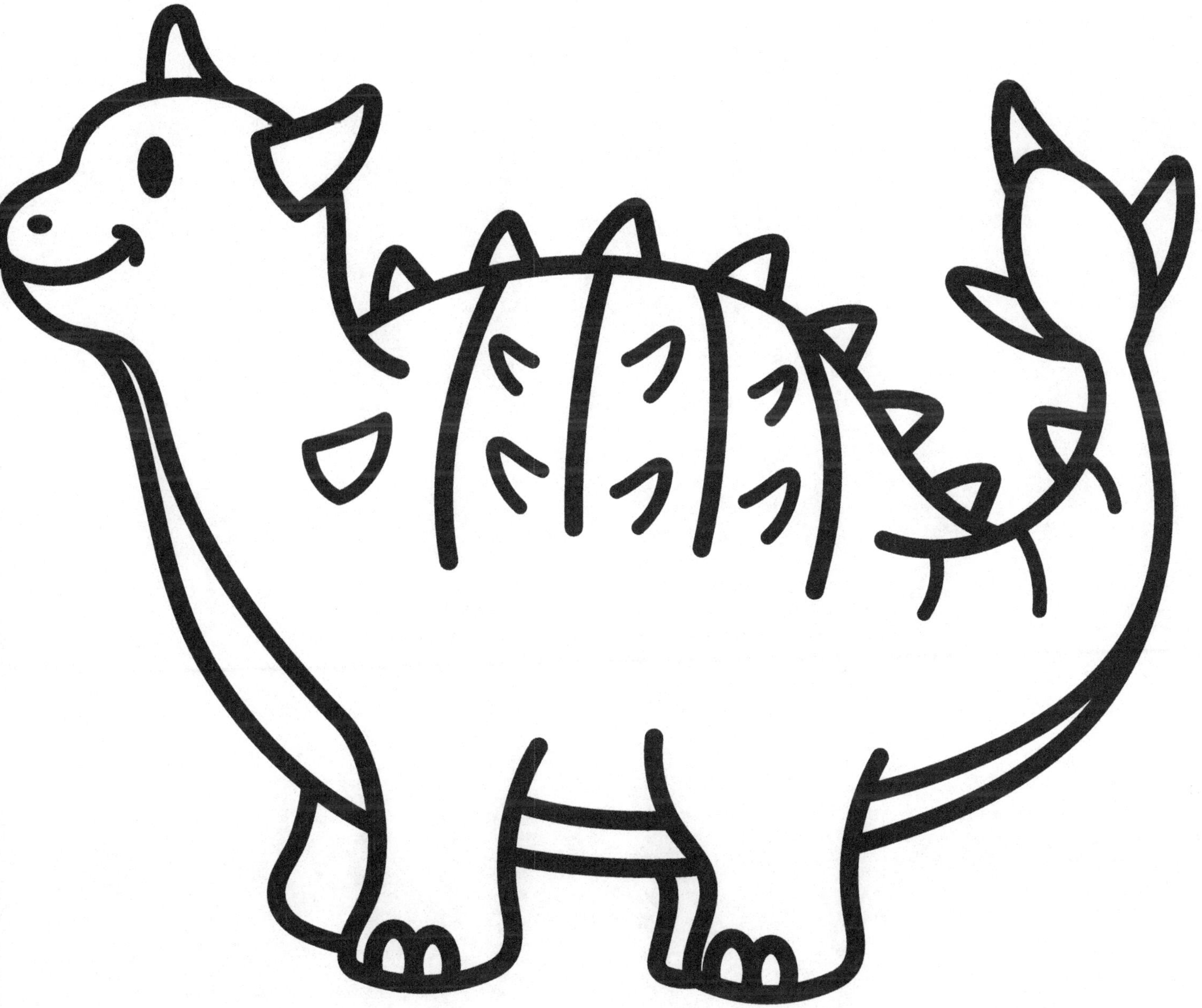

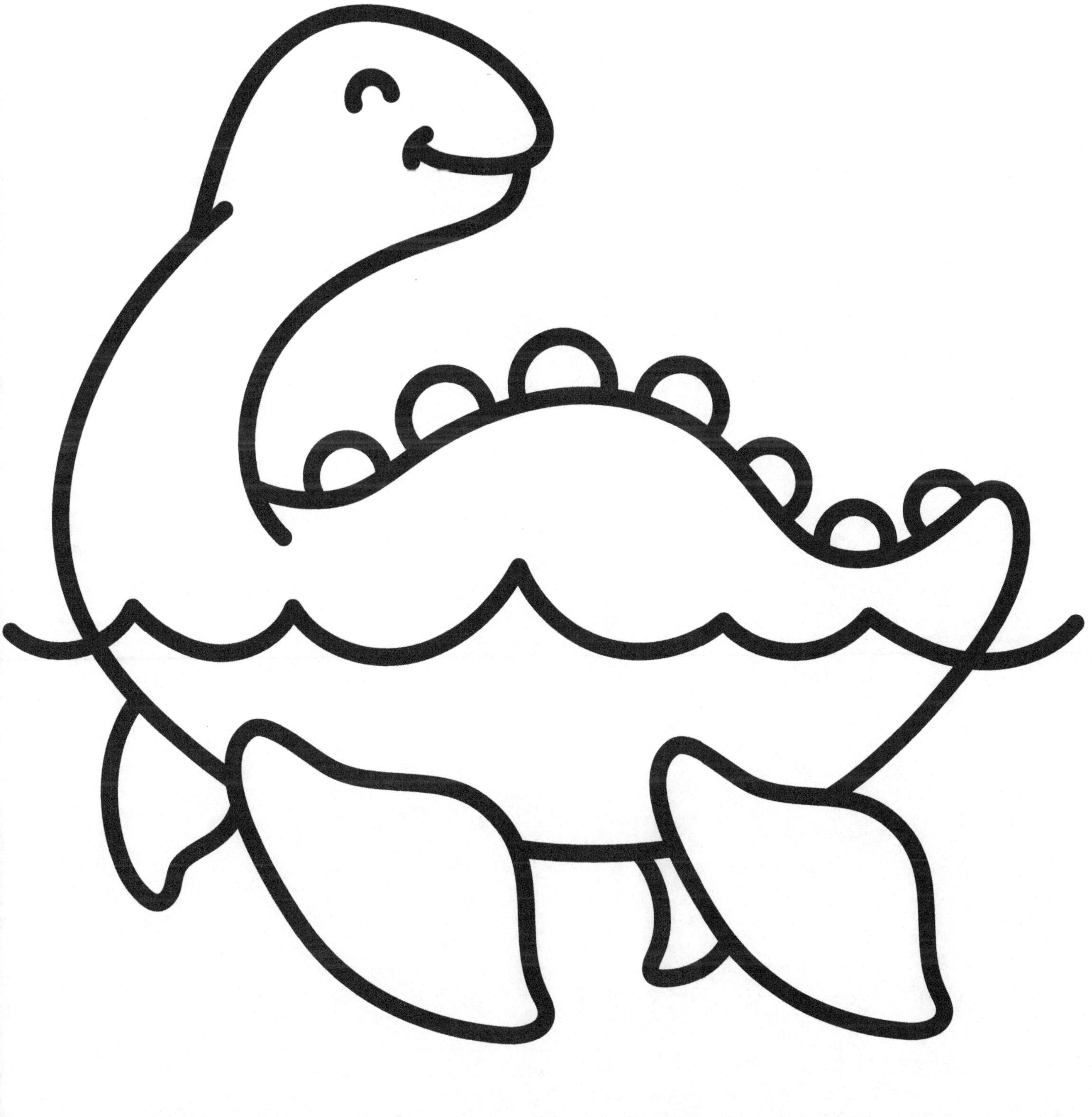

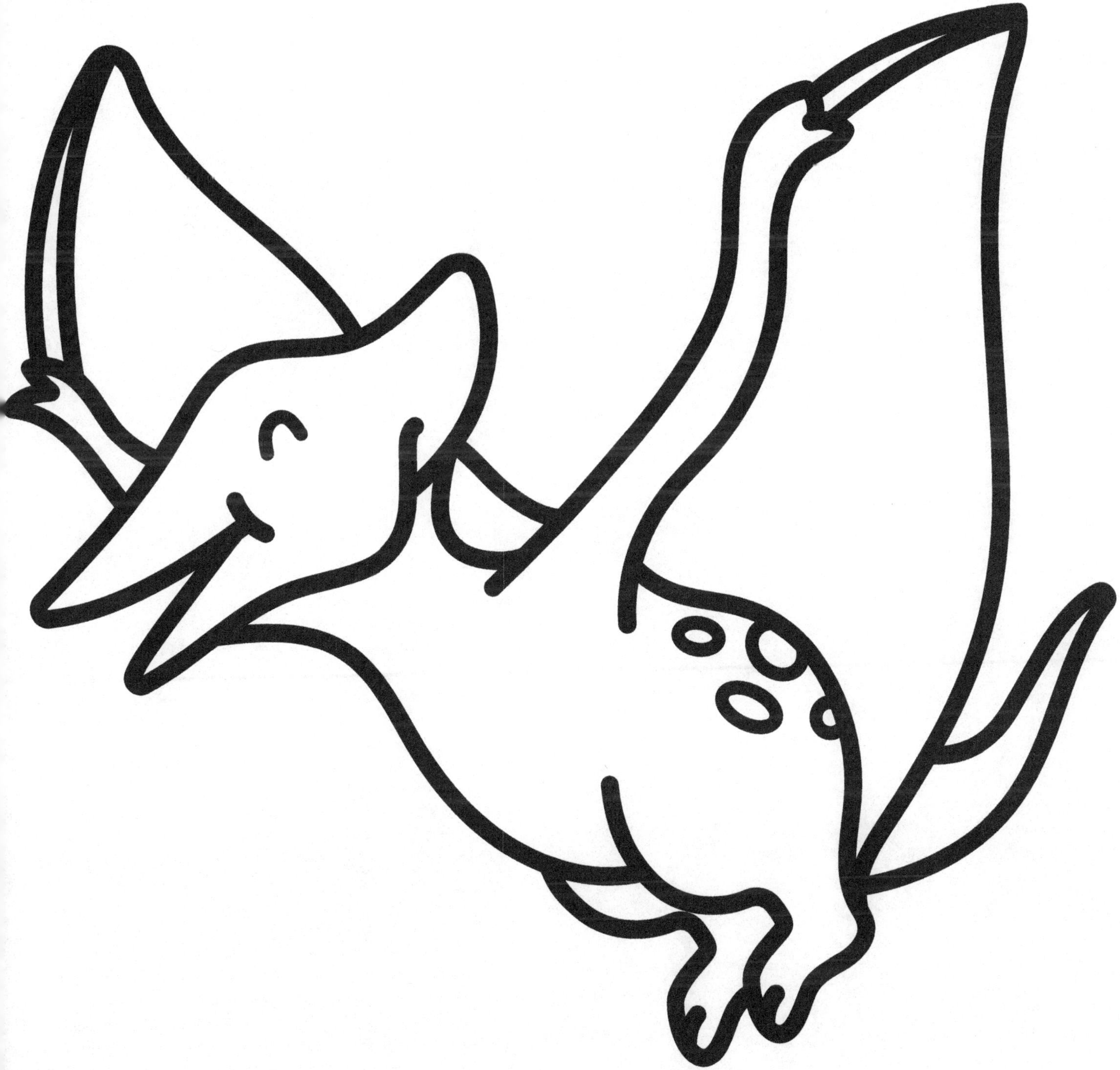

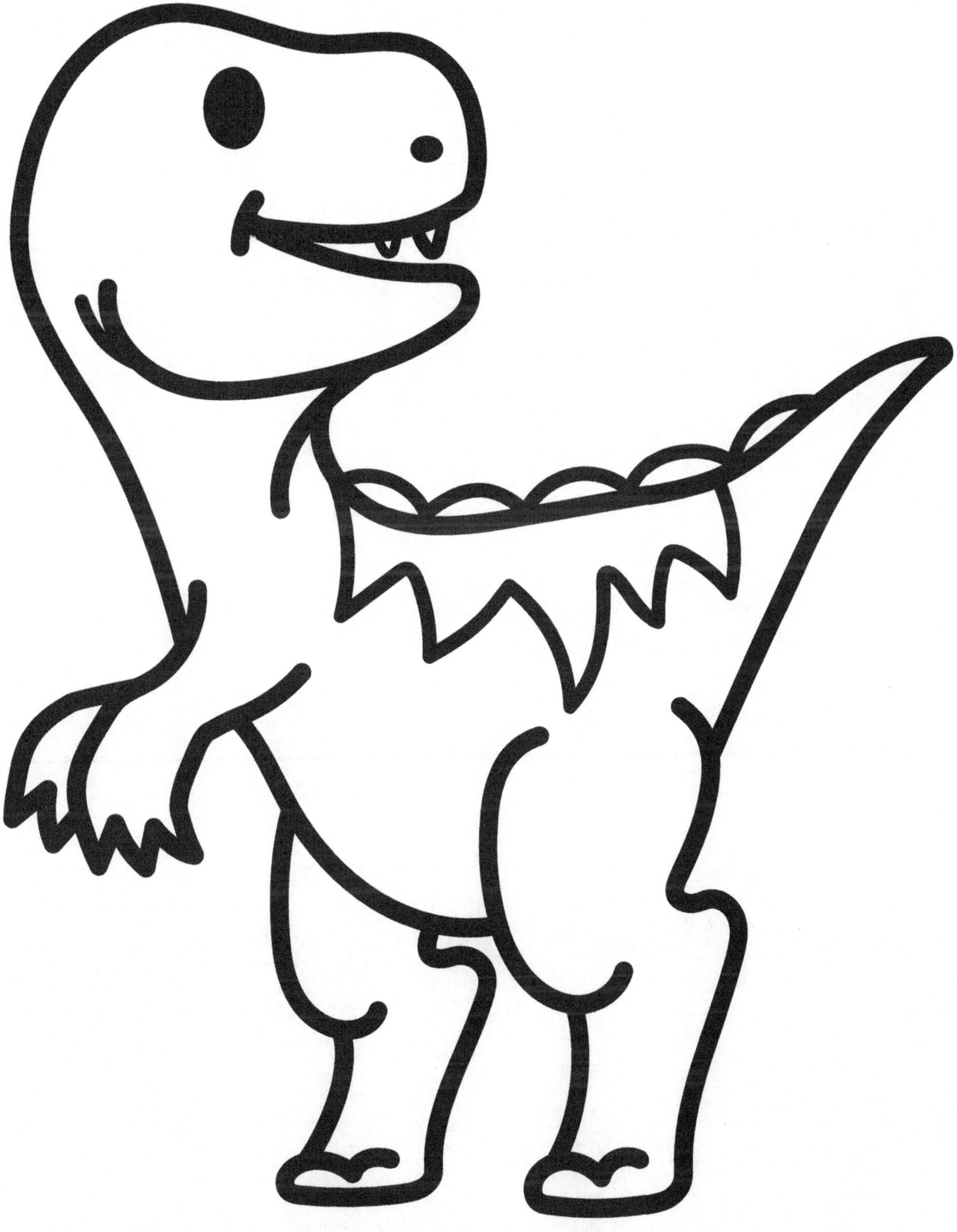

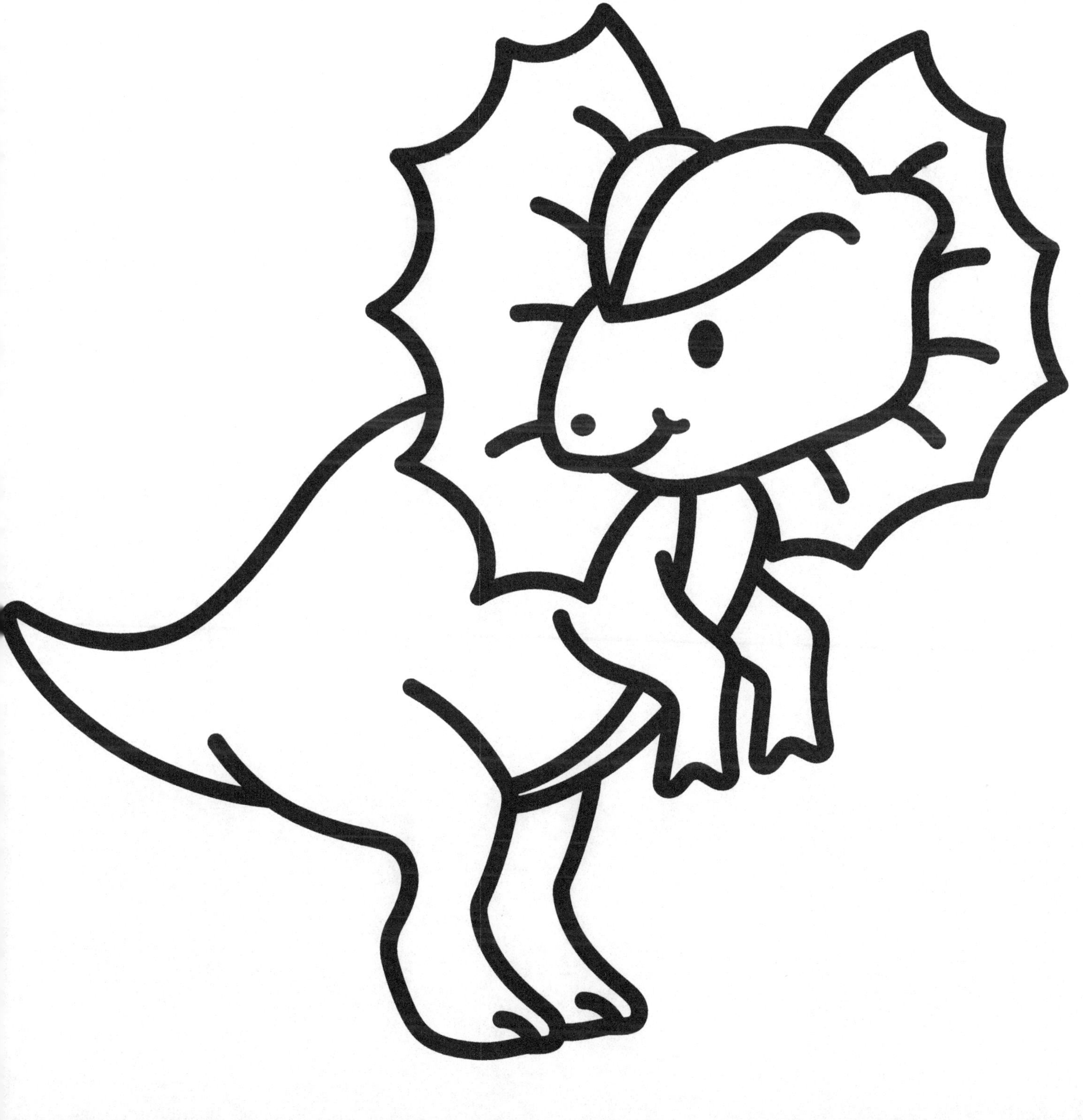

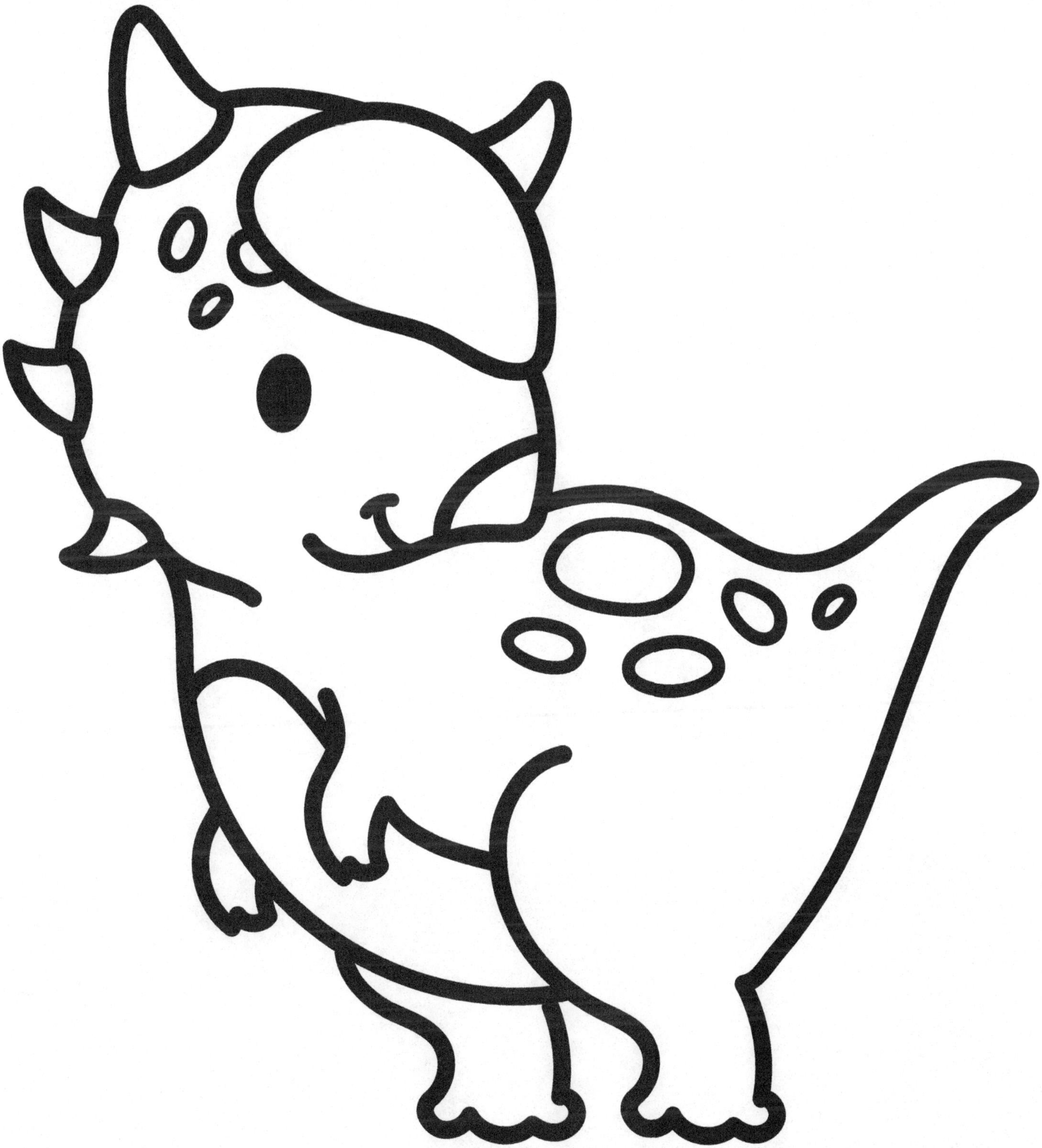

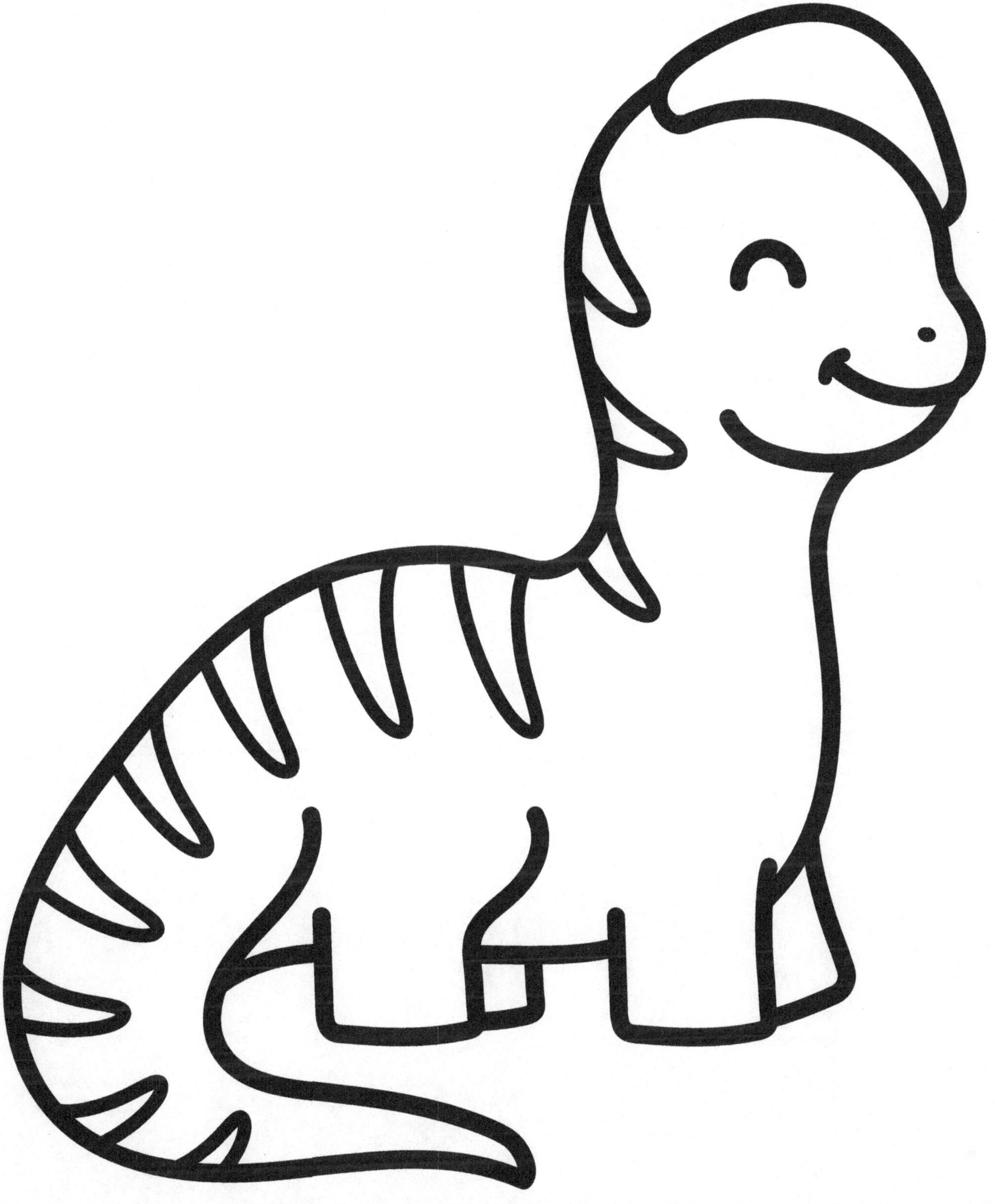

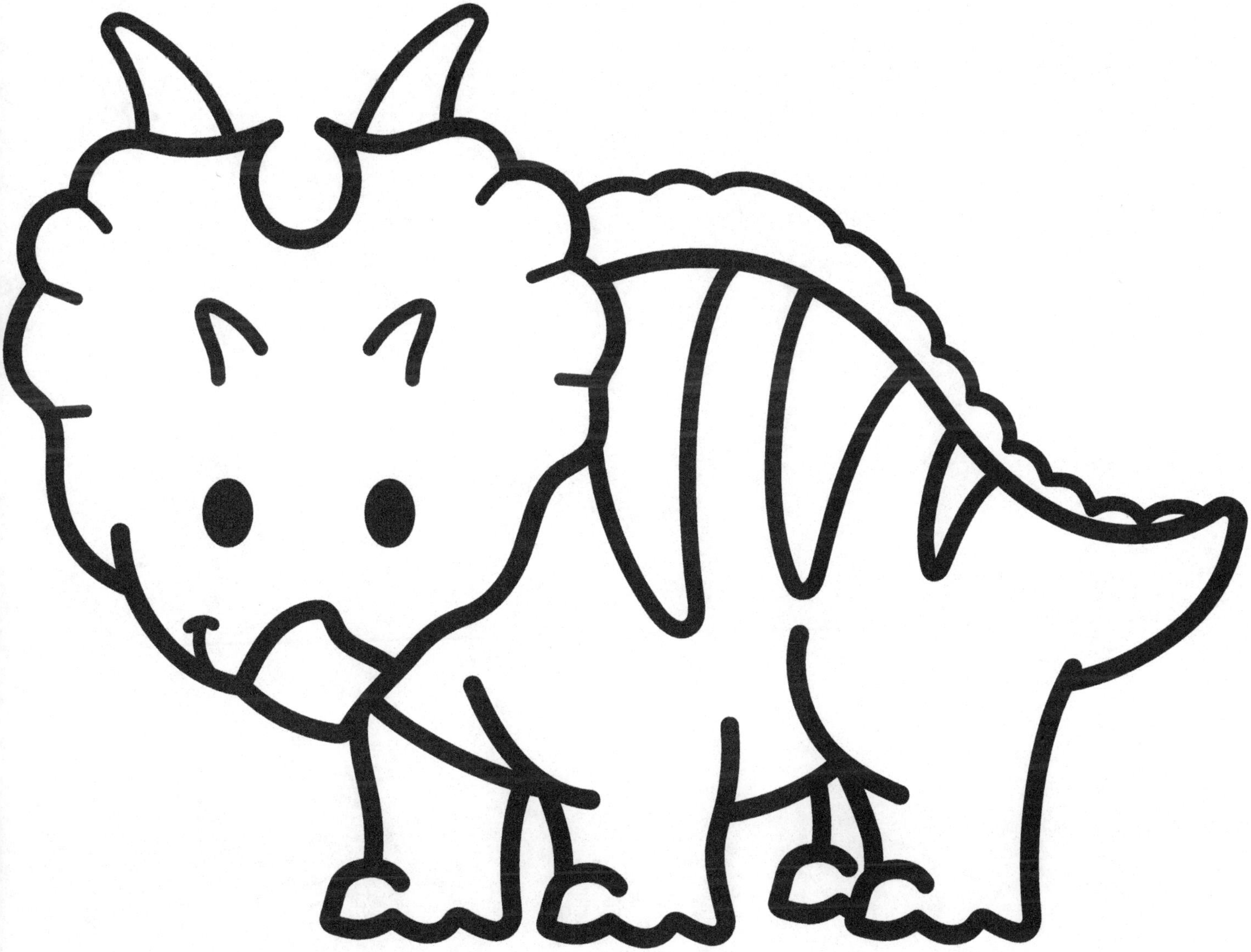

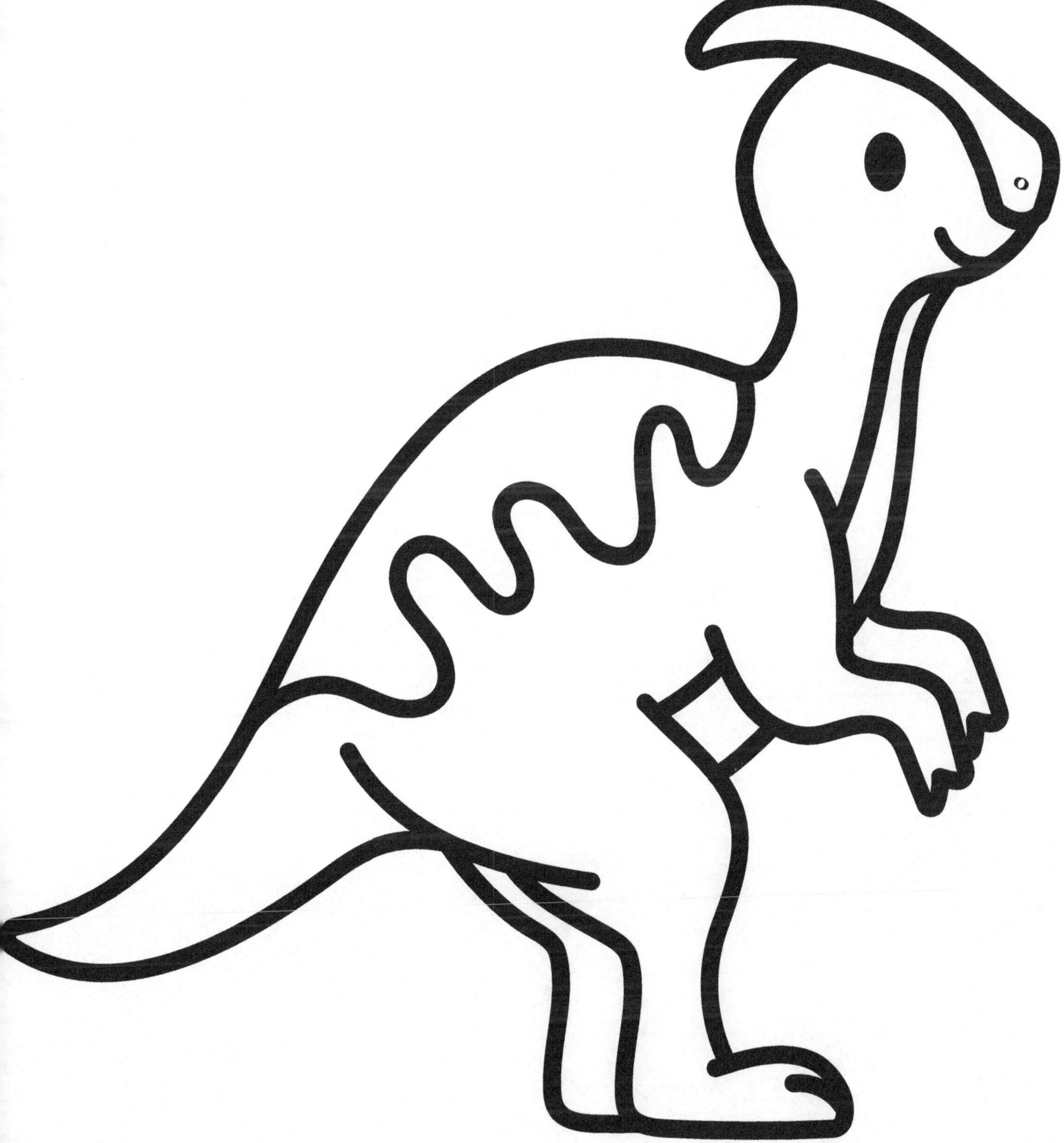

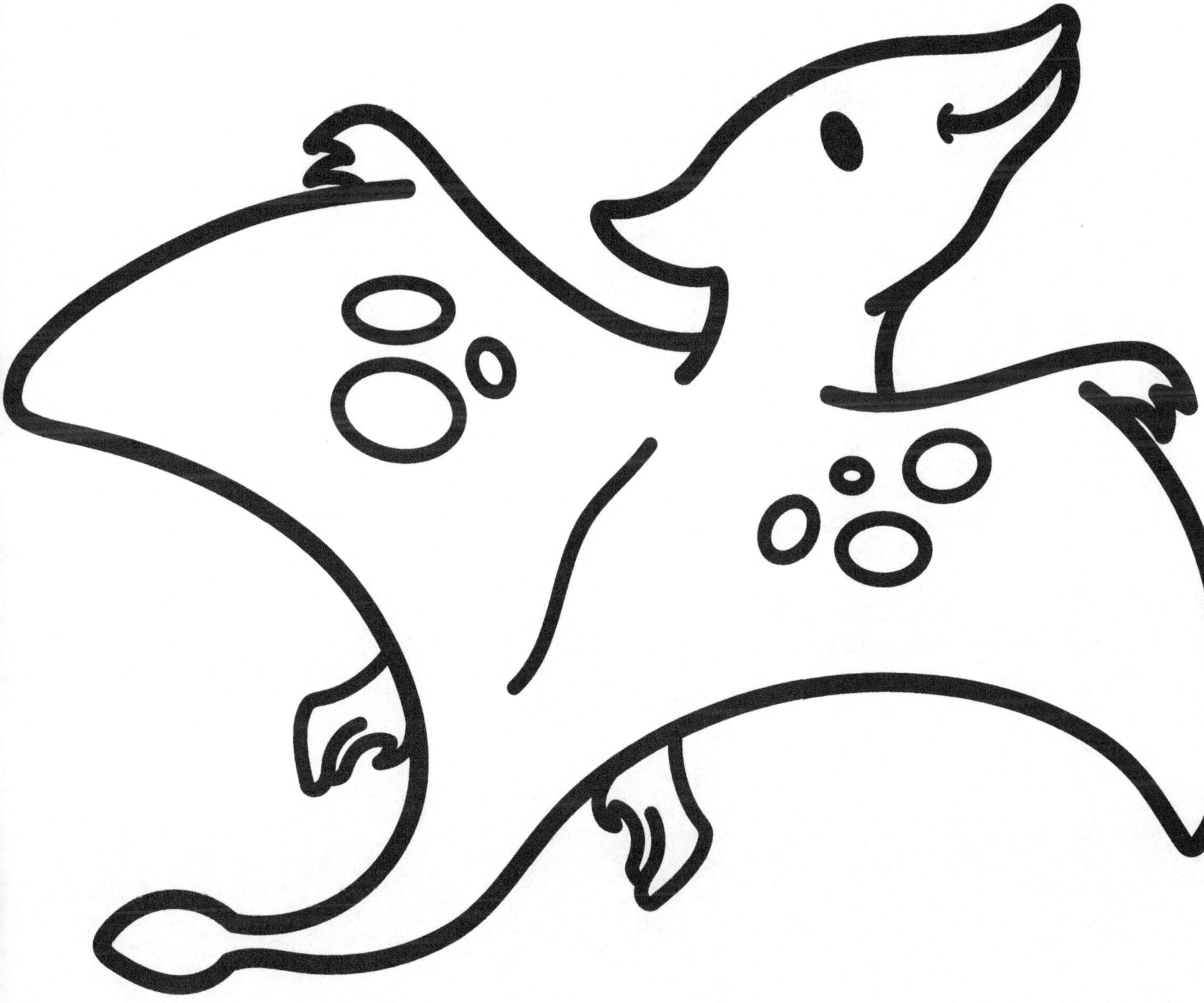

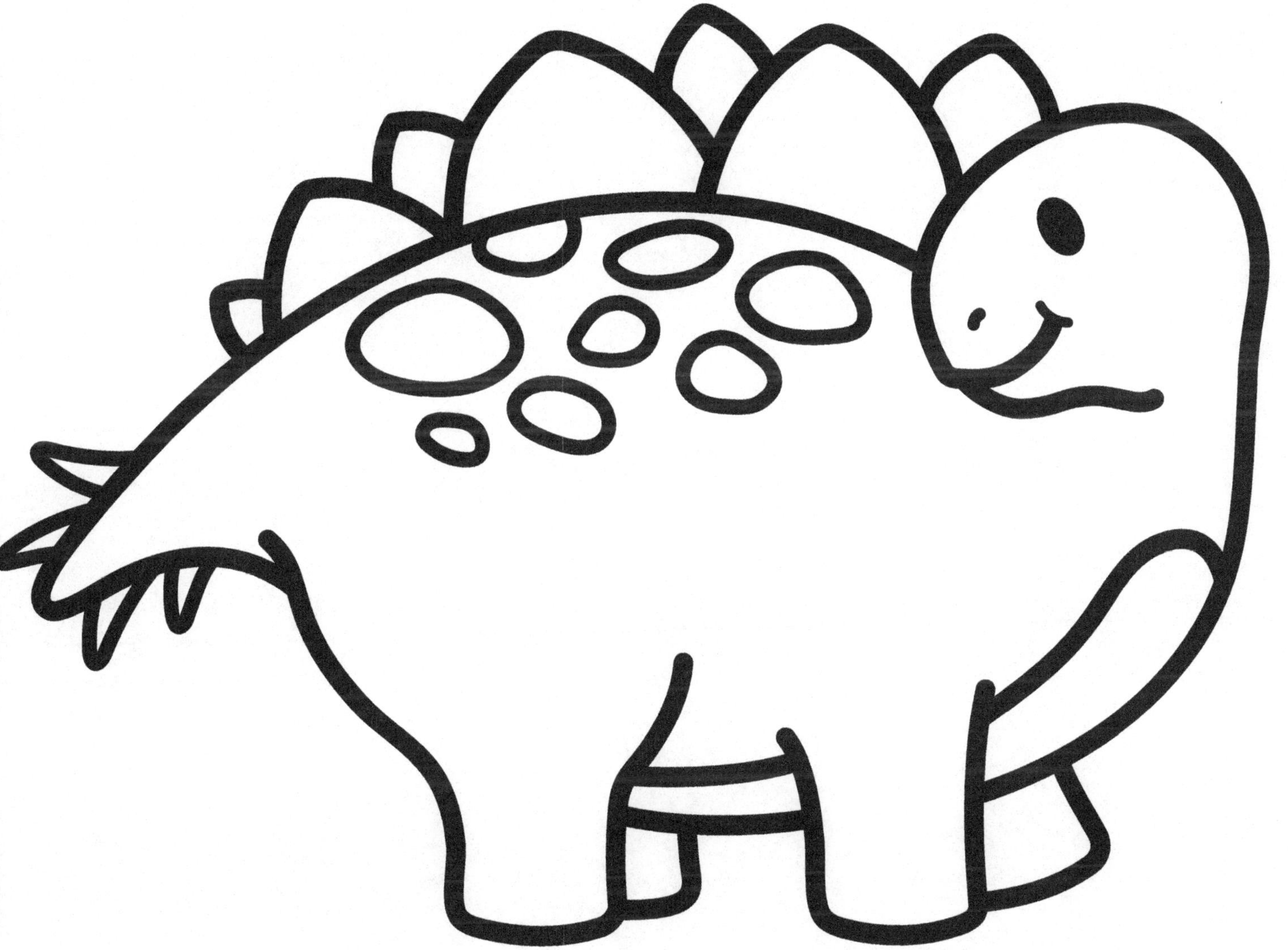

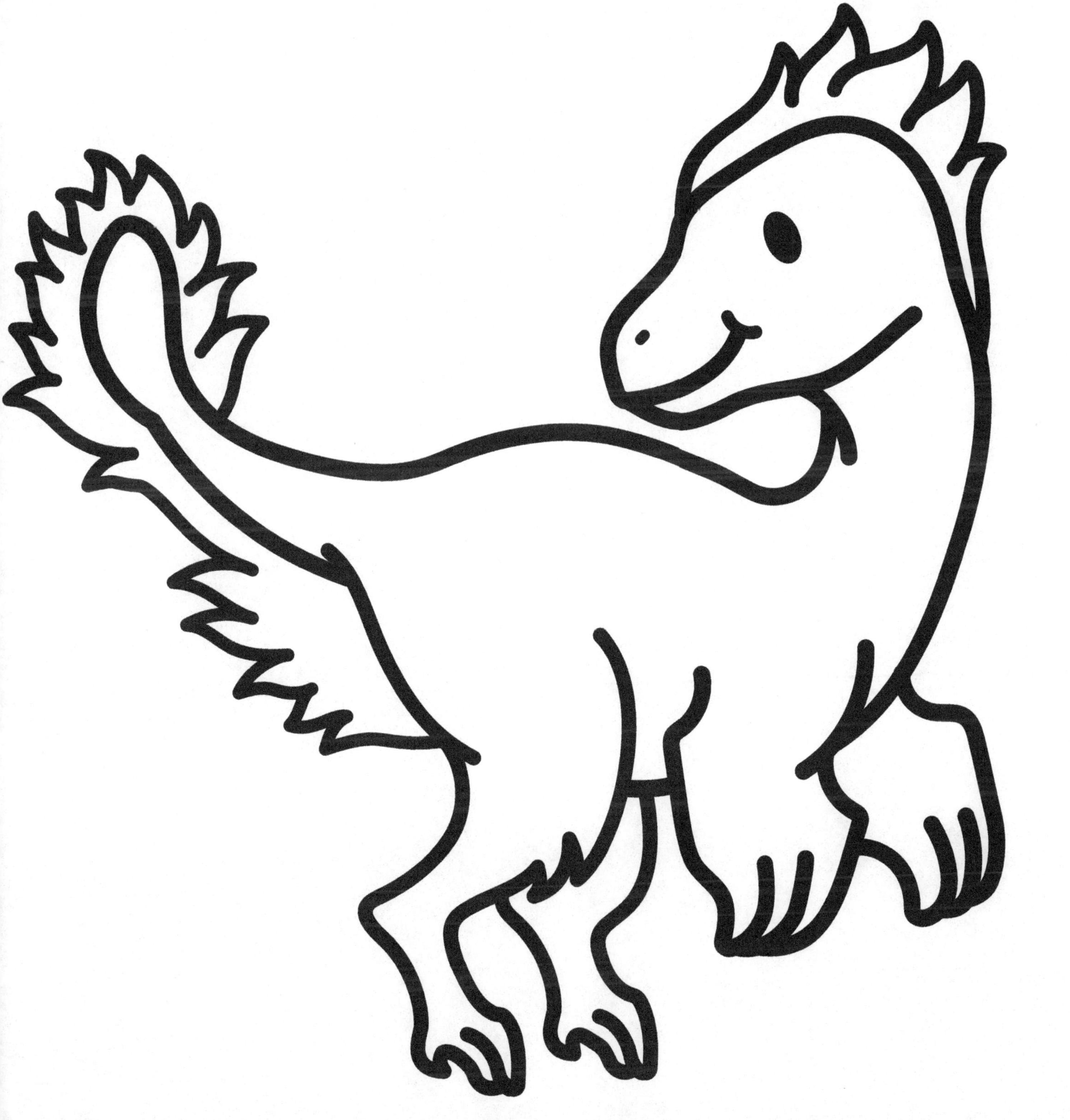

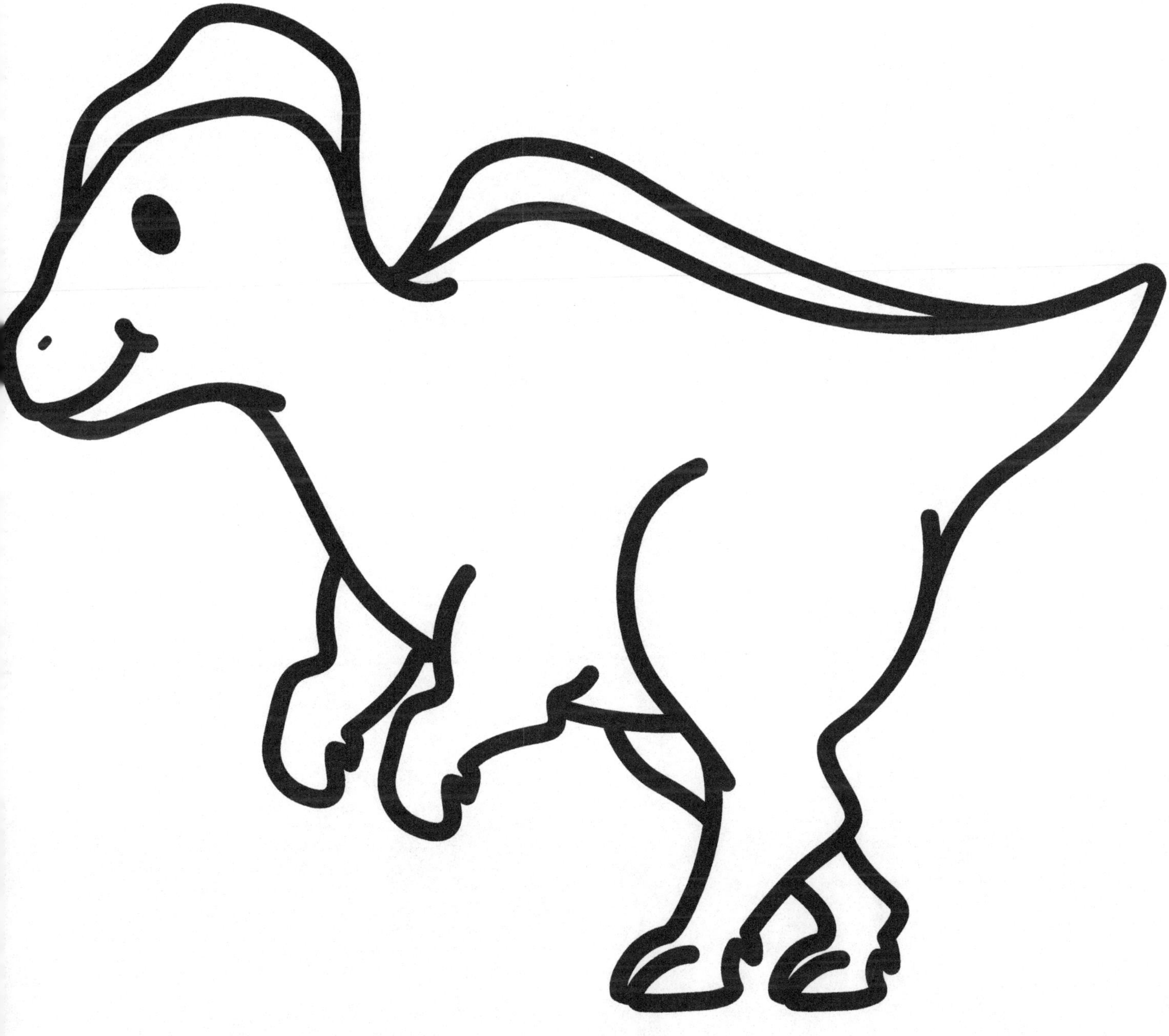

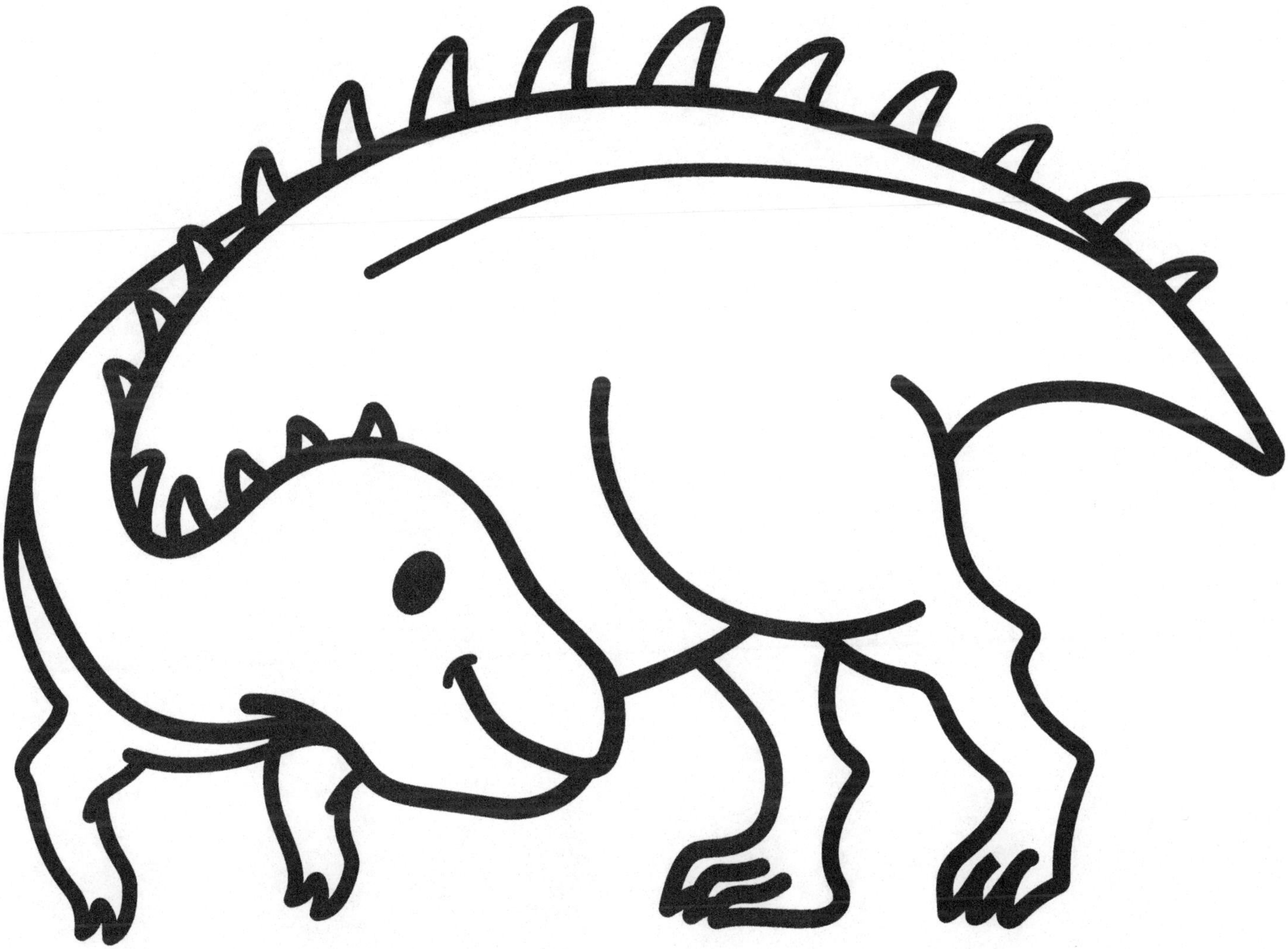

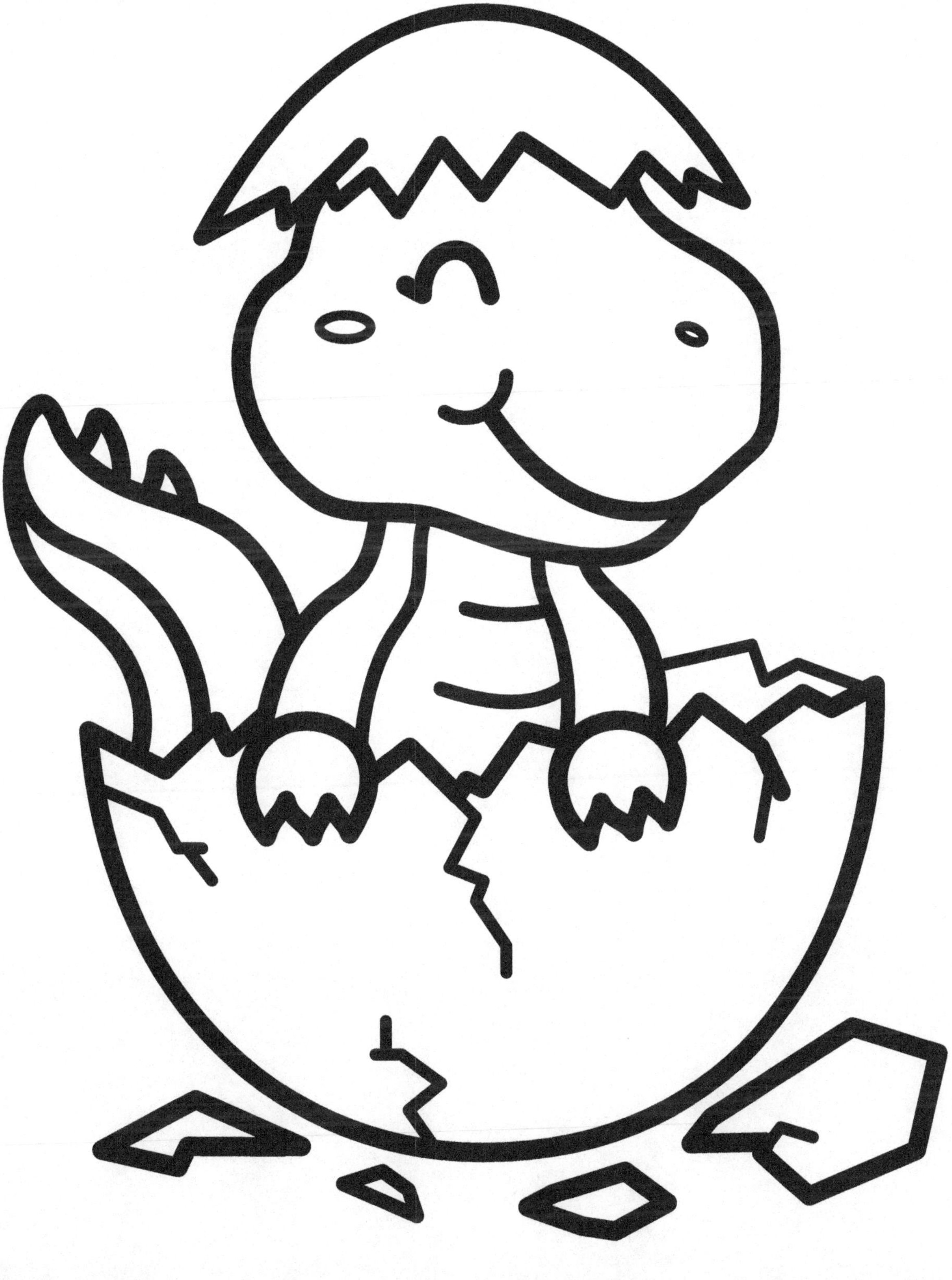

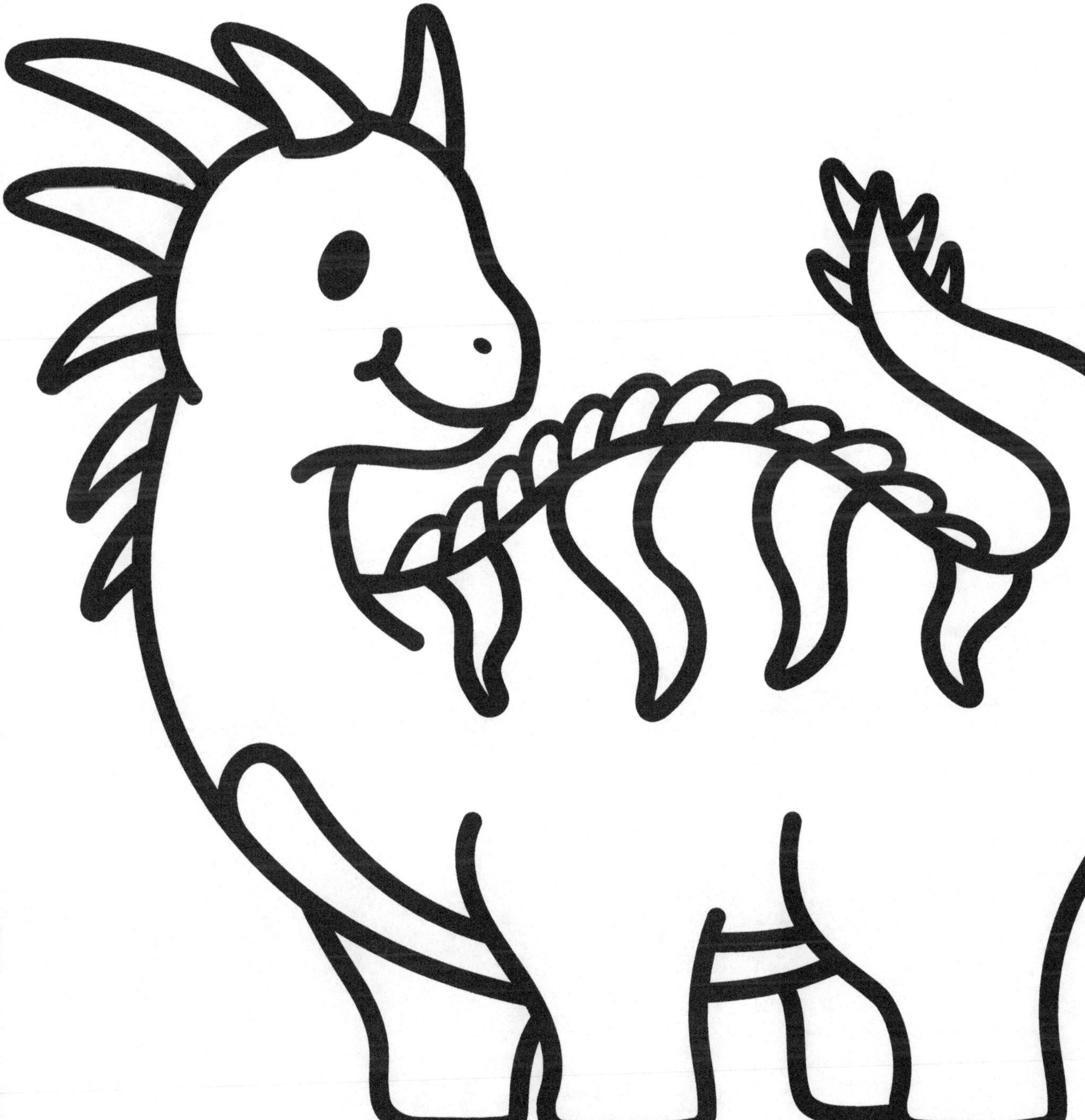

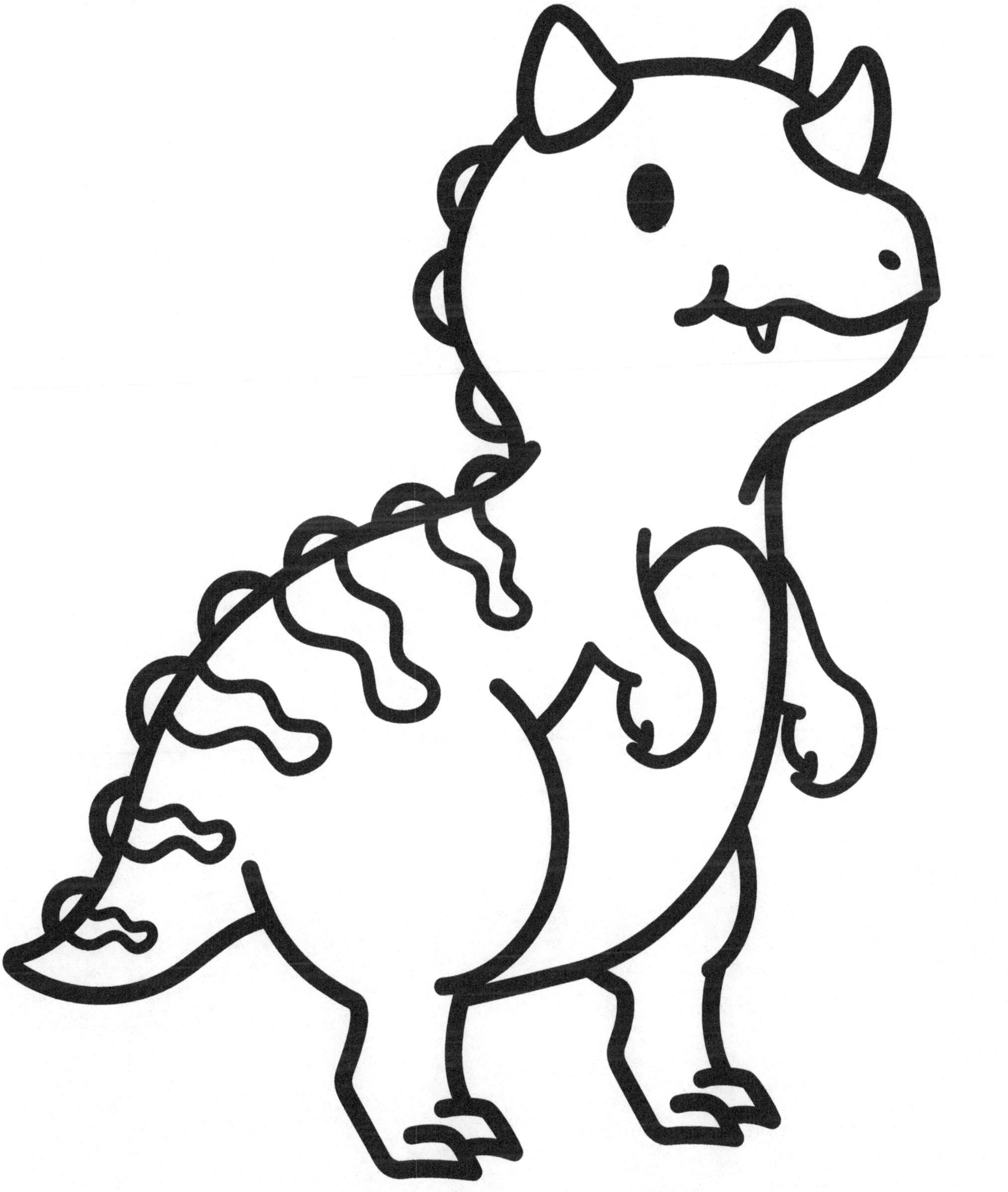

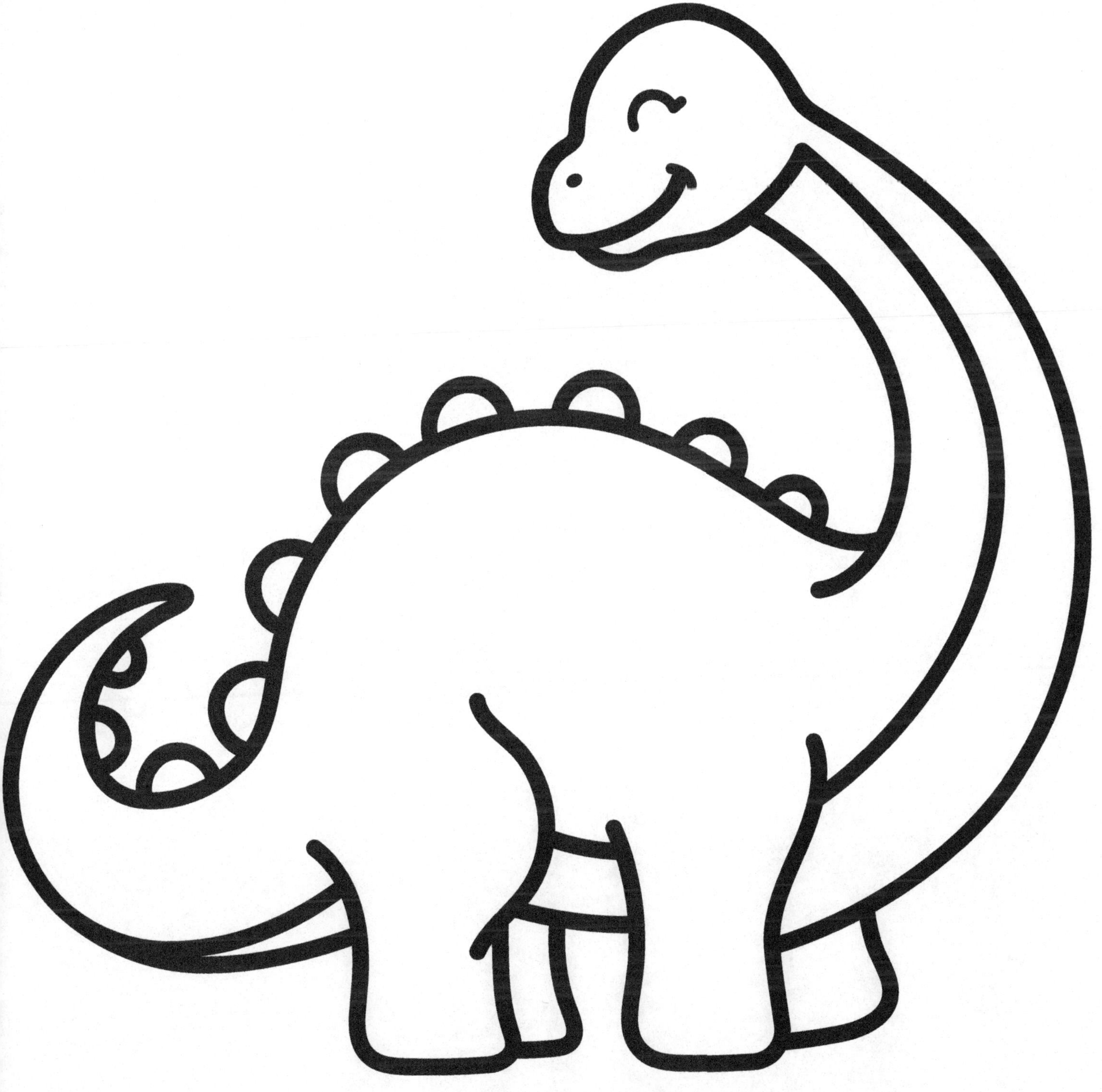

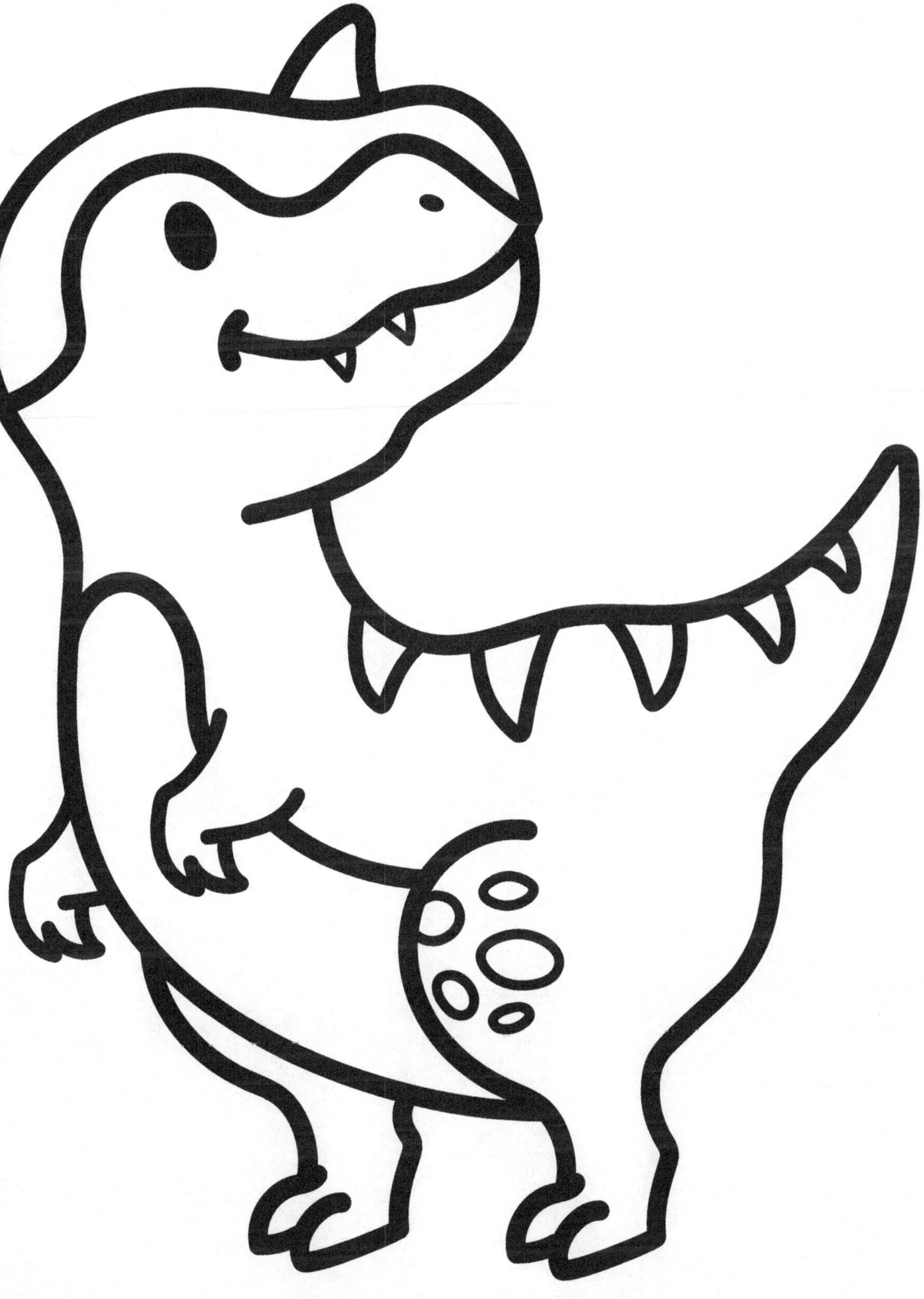

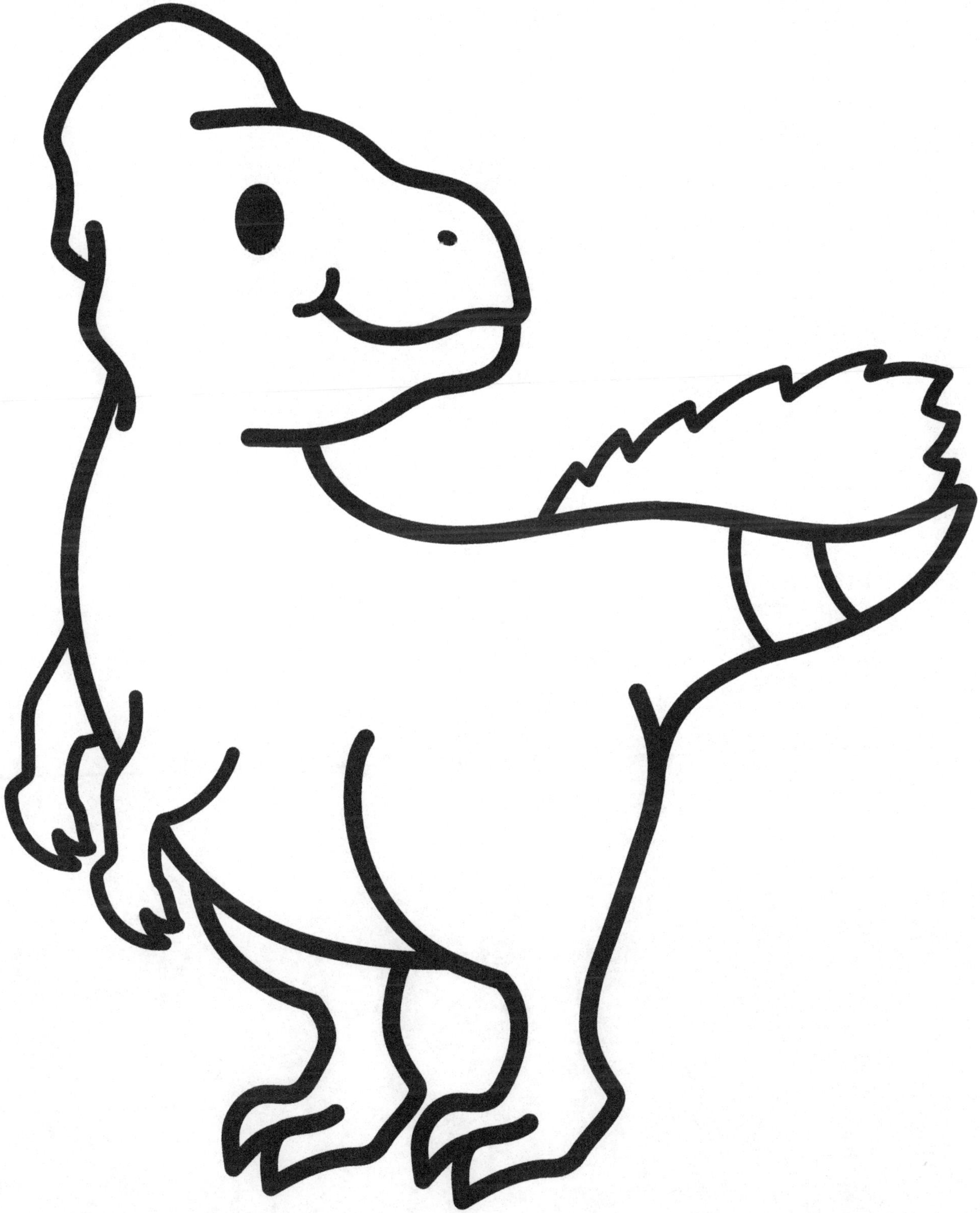

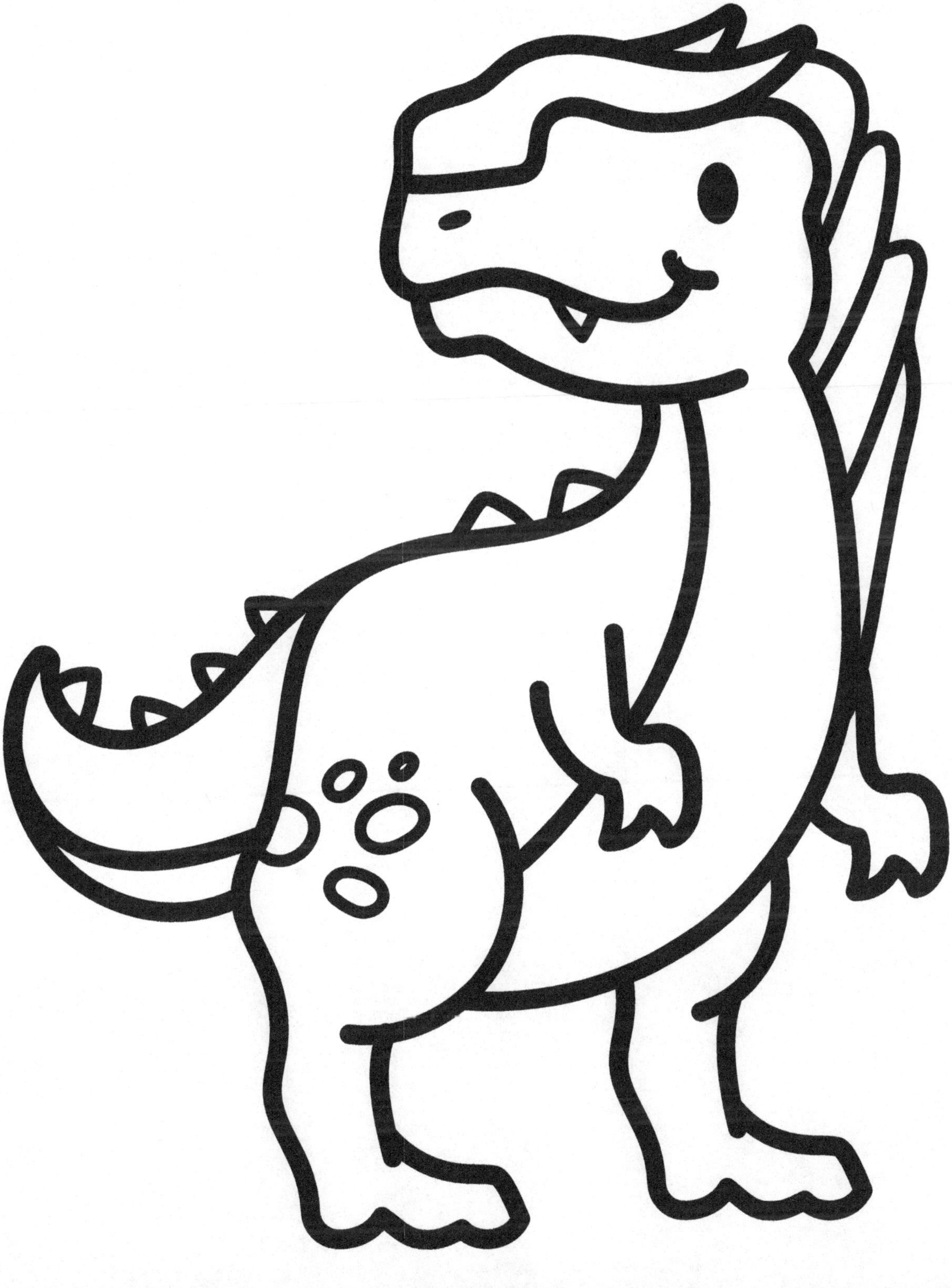

☆☆☆☆☆

We hope you liked this book! It would mean a lot to us to receive feedback in form of a rating on Amazon or via e-mail at booksbykwabu@gmail.com.

Don't forget to scan the QR-Code below or visit kwabu.com to download your free coloring book!

@booksbykwabu @booksbykwabu

THANK YOU!

:-)

ISBN: 979-8453810116

© 2023 Kwabu LLC - All rights reserved

Imprint:
Kwabu LLC
Attn: Wes Holmstrom
PO Box 1023
Refugio, TX 78377

Made in United States
North Haven, CT
30 June 2024